JOSE CABRERA PRESENTS

THE PREMiERE CRYiNG MACHO MAN COLLECTiON
PRiME CUT

BY JOSE CABRERA

uPandover publishing

DEDICATED
TO MY WIFE,
NAOMI
FOR BELIEVING

THANKS TO JOE SHARPNACK, TOM SMITH, DAVID TUCKER, JEFF COOK, ALEX DIAZ, JAVIER HERNANDEZ, SCOTT TOBIN, AARON NORHANIAN, DAMON CART, GREG AND OLIVIA CLAYTON, MATTHEW THOMAS, CLAIRE TELLING, CHERYL FELDMAN, GREG SMITH, LIZ AND RYAN MAAS, KEITH KNIGHT, ERIC TUCKER, THOMAS HUNTINGTON, MADHAPPYS, PAUL INGRAM, JAMIE LEO, JON AND MERCH RUBACH, JADELYN VALENZUELA, CARA QUINN, WILL TUCKER, STEPHEN BAUM, JOYSETTE CABRERA, NOAH VALENZUELA, MIGUEL PEREZ, BENNY BEAR, ANNIE TUCKER, CUZ, ANITA AND ALAN, ERIN DOYLE, MARIROSE OCCHIOGROSSO, ELAINE BAGORIO, GRANT KIRKPATRICK, PRAIRIE LIGHTS, CHRIS SHIELDS AND TO ALL OF MY DEAR READERS WHO HAVE TOLERATED ME IN THEIR INBOXES. THANK YOU, THANK YOU!

POST OFFICE BOX 5313
PLAYA DEL REY, CA 90296 U.S.A
JOSE@CRYINGMACHOMAN.COM

IF YOU'D LIKE TO KEEP UP WITH THE LATEST CRYING MACHO MAN CARTOONS, PLEASE VISIT:
WWW.CRYINGMACHOMAN.COM
TO ORDER BOOKS PLEASE EMAIL: SALES@CRYINGMACHOMAN.COM

ISBN-10 0-9792854-0-2
ISBN-13 978-0-9792854-0-0

FORWARD COURTESY OF JOE SHARPNACK

COVER DESIGN: JOSE CABRERA

INTRO

First things first, if you're holding this book, **YOU'RE NOT NORMAL!**
But I mean that in the best way, because you want more than just **ZAP,**
CRACK or **POW** from your cartoons. You want funny strips that'll make you
bust out laughing but also make you think. I know I do, and that's one of the
main reasons I created Crying Macho Man.

The other reason is 'cause I can't help myself. I **LOVE** creating cartoons.
Have since I was a wee lad. Back in grade school, my friends would always
ask me to draw the teacher in some compromising position. The drawings
usually ended up in the dean's office along with my ass. But I didn't care.
I was addicted to the racket it caused. Now I'm all grown up and I'm still
causing a racket, but instead of getting sent to the dean's office, I'm
out on the couch.

I hope you enjoy watching a grown man cry!

Much love,

Jose aka Crying Macho Man

FORWARD

I've been in the political cartoon business for a long time and have always been willing to encourage and/or dare anyone who professes the need to speak their mind to do so. But to do it so as many possible can hear.

Anyone can spew their socio/political "expertise" from the highest barstool in Topeka while knowing full well that they are in the relative comfort and safety of a familiar environment. It's when those arguments are thought through carefully, put to paper and then published with a name on them is where the risks are taken. You can be pummeled with a mountain of shit (believe me, I know) for bringing up uncomfortable truths in a mass forum. Not everyone has the gut for it. Apparently Cabrera does, so I say run with it.

It takes a lot to get a Macho Man to cry, but when he does, heed his wails for he must have something to cry about.

JOE SHARPNACK, 2007
WWW.SHARPTOONS.COM

CRYING MACHO MAN
BY JOSÉ CABRERA

ARM WRESTLE YOUR SOUL

CRYING MACHO MAN
BY JOSÉ CABRERA

CHANGE ME BACK

I'M LOVIN' IT

BURGER ACTUAL SIZE...CAUSE JESUS GETS WHAT THE **HELL** HE WANTS!

CRYING MACHO MAN
BY JOSÉ CABRERA

DR. PHIL VS DNA

CRYING MACHO MAN
BY JOSÉ CABRERA

GRAFITTI

FIDEL AND TONY

CRYING MACHO MAN
BY JOSÉ CABRERA

DR. PHIL VS TOM CRUISE

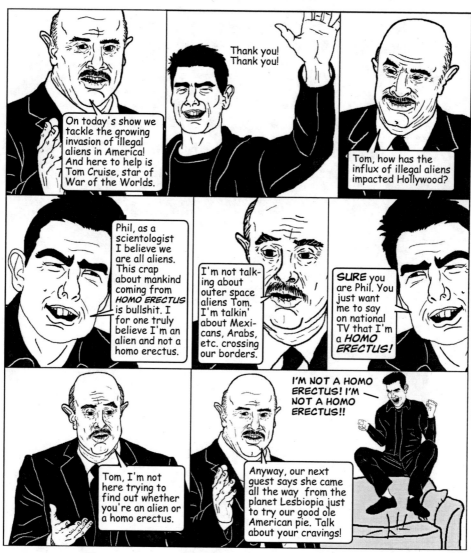

Thank you! Thank you!

On today's show we tackle the growing invasion of illegal aliens in America! And here to help is Tom Cruise, star of War of the Worlds.

Tom, how has the influx of illegal aliens impacted Hollywood?

Phil, as a scientologist I believe we are all aliens. This crap about mankind coming from *HOMO ERECTUS* is bullshit. I for one truly believe I'm an alien and not a homo erectus.

I'm not talking about outer space aliens Tom. I'm talkin' about Mexicans, Arabs, etc. crossing our borders.

SURE you are Phil. You just want me to say on national TV that I'm a *HOMO ERECTUS!*

Tom, I'm not here trying to find out whether you're an alien or a homo erectus.

I'M NOT A HOMO ERECTUS! I'M NOT A HOMO ERECTUS!!

Anyway, our next guest says she came all the way from the planet Lesbiopia just to try our good ole American pie. Talk about your cravings!

FIN

FOXY

HEART ATTACK MAN SEZ

¡Yo Quiero Ambulance!

ALITO'S WAY

CLOSE SHAVE

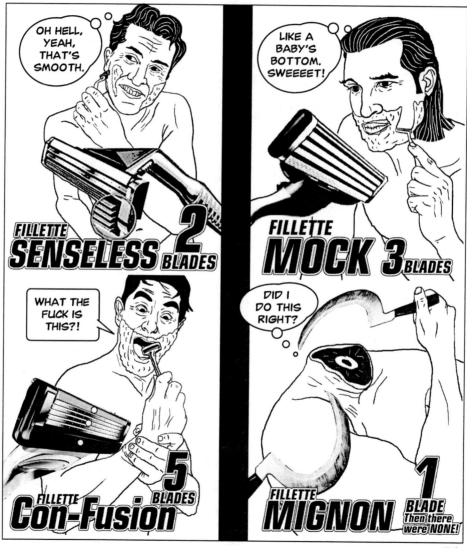

FIN

CRYING MACHO MAN
BY JOSÉ CABRERA

CASTRO CAN'T GET NETFLIX

PRINCE AND THE REVOLUTIONARY

SPLINGO

CRYING MACHO MAN
BY JOSÉ CABRERA

DIAL 911 FOR FREEDOM

Panel 1: My fellow Americans, I have thought long and hard about the eventfulness after 9/11. We all sufferized this in cumbered. And I'm here to explain my theorization.

Panel 2: We have strong intel to back up my informed and difficult theory 'sigh'...and hard work it was...

Panel 3: Did you know that 911 is almost the same as 411, except for one number...just one...

Panel 4: ...and 411 stands for information...**FREE** information ripe for any terrorist to pick with their evil terrorist hands for eviling duties.

Panel 5: ...so what I am propositionizing is that we change 411 to 911. And when terrorist come a callin' for FREE info... they're gonna get an ear full of emergency operators.

Panel 6: So from now on dial 411 for emergencies and ringerize 911 for '**FREE'DOM** info!

FIN

CRYING MACHO MAN
BY JOSÉ CABRERA

GRIZZLY FUTURE

FIN

CRYING MACHO MAN
BY JOSÉ CABRERA

WANTED: AN ALMIGHTY GOD

CRYING MACHO MAN
BY JOSÉ CABRERA

VEAL

FIN

CRYING MACHO MAN
BY JOSÉ CABRERA

THE KBA

FIN

CRYING MACHO MAN
BY JOSÉ CABRERA

CROCODILE TEARS

CRYING MACHO MAN
BY JOSÉ CABRERA

THE MASTER'S CARD

I'LL PASS

FIN

MY TIGHT BUSINESS CARD GIVING STYLE

KONICHIWA.

KONICHI-WHAT?! YO, THIS MU FUCKA IS CRAZY. ANYWAY MY CARD GIVING STYLE IS OFF THE HOOK! HE WON'T KNOW WHAT HIT HIM. THAT'S RIGHT, SNATCH THAT SHIT UP.

...YEAH. YO THAT BITCH TOOK MY CARD. **WORD!** I LIKE BOWED AND THEN HE SAID SOME CRAZY VOODOO SHIT. BUT I KEPT MYSELF REAL COOL. YUP! TWO HANDS! AHHHHH THAT'S RIGHT FUCKA-YOU HEARD ME. **TWO HANDS!!**

33

PUBLIC SERVICE ANNOUNCEMENT

THE BRAIN GRILL

MAKING COPIES

FIN

CRYING MACHO MAN
BY JOSÉ CABRERA

IRONIC CHEF

FIN

HUGO AND THE POPE

FIN

CRYING MACHO MAN
BY JOSÉ CABRERA

OFF STAR

CHARLIE AND KIEFER PART I

FIN

CHARLIE AND KIEFER PART 2

FIN

REDUCTO

CRYING MACHO MAN
BY JOSÉ CABRERA

CHARLIE AND OLD DIRTY BASTARD

FIN

CRYING MACHO MAN
BY JOSÉ CABRERA

GULLIBLE COPS

FIN

AL GORE TELLS IT LIKE IT IS

FIN

DR PHIL, WE NEED HELP!

FIN

MARK FOLEY'S CAREER CHANGE

BANANA REPUBLICAN

CRYING MACHO MAN
BY JOSÉ CABRERA

THE STUTTERING PIMP

FIN

THE MEXICAN DEPOT

CONT.

MOX NEWS CHANNEL

On todays shows

The O' Reilly Factor: Mexicans should go back to Africa.

Ann Coulter: Contracts rare shit mouth disease.

Geraldo: Still covering Katrina story.

Hannity & Colmes: We still support our white troops!

SPECIAL REPORT

Crocodiles lobby to become new Republican mascot.
Eat elephant to prove point.

FIN

WHAT'S ON YOUR MIND ARNOLD?

I understand what it is to be **WEAK** and **POOR.** I feel compassion for all immigrants.

I **COME** from a compassionate society that **DOESN'T** believe in the death penalty.

...as far as family is concerned-I am faithful and loyal as all Californians should be.

I have listened to Tookie Williams plea for clemency and I'm having to make the hardest decision of my life.

FIN

WHO YOU ROLL WITH?

FIN

MINDY THE TELEMARKETER

VAMPU-CHEK™

RETURN POLICY

CONT.

FIN

THIS OLD CRAP

CRYING MACHO MAN
BY JOSÉ CABRERA

BOOTY CALL

CRYING MACHO MAN
BY JOSÉ CABRERA

BROKEN PROMISED LAND

BUSH HAS STERN WORDS FOR CHINA

FIN

CRYING MACHO MAN
BY JOSÉ CABRERA

EARLY SIGNS OF A MIDLIFE CRISIS

KEEP IT TOGETHER GREG OLD BOY. JUS' CAUSE YOU'RE 36 TODAY DON'T MEAN YOU AIN'T STILL GOT IT!

NOW GO OUT THERE LIKE THE STUD YOU ARE AND GET THAT GIRL...AND DON'T **BLOW IT!**

IS SHE TRYING TO LEAVE?

UHM, IS THERE ANYTHING I CAN OFFER YOU...BEER, WINE, WATER, AIR...

FIN

SADAAM DON'T CARE

FIN

PRAY FER ME

HOT DOG EATING CONTEST

FIN

CRYING MACHO MAN

BY JOSÉ CABRERA

ILLEGAL ALIEN

CRYING MACHO MAN
BY JOSÉ CABRERA

INTERNET PREDATORS

FIN

CRYING MACHO MAN

BY JOSÉ CABRERA

AHHH-MEN

Mariah Cries Over Starving Kids

"Whenever I watch TV and see those poor starving kids all over the world, I can't help but cry. I mean I'd like to be skinny like that but not with all those flies and death and stuff."

- Mariah Carey

CRYING MACHO MAN
BY JOSÉ CABRERA

FIST FULL OF PENNIES

COJUMBO

FIN

CRYING MACHO MAN
BY JOSÉ CABRERA

HAPPY BIRTHDAY MR. POPE

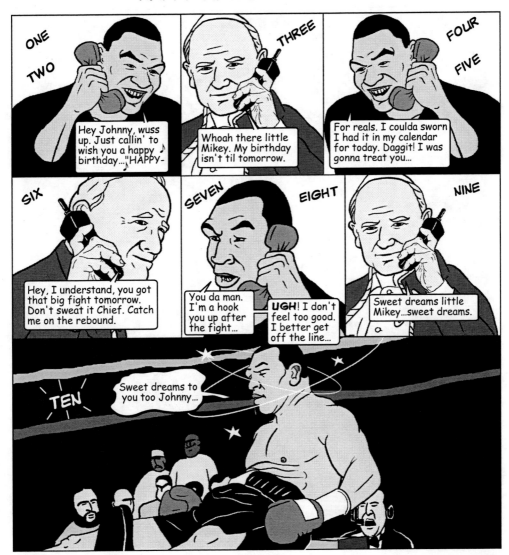

FIN

MINDY THE TELEMARKETER MEETS DRACULA

CRYING MACHO MAN
BY JOSÉ CABRERA

PROFILED

FIN

CASTRO'S DILEMMA

Che? Waddup-where you been? Tryin' ta call you. My Xbox is all hot and shit...I'm stuck again. This time on level eight. How do I get past the fire golem?

...com'on Fidel. You gotta use the ice sword. **THINK!** Make sure you take the amulet when you defeat him or you won't be able to go onto the next level.

True dat. All right dude. I gotta get back to slashing throats and conquering the Nosgarth empire. Peace out.

A FEW HOURS LATER

Dude. I messed up. I forgot to take the amulet. You were right. Shit! I had to start all over again.

Duuuuude! Why don't you just get the cheat codes online. I don't know why you waste your time on RPG games. I'll lend you Halo. It's tight...

Na-na. I don't like shoot 'em ups. I like to plan and strategize. Man, my eyes are killin' me. So wha'choo doing?

Jus' tryin' ta make a peanut butter and jelly sandwich, but it's the natural kind with the oil at the top. I'm just gonna buy Skippy from now on.

Yo don't be feeding the big corporate machines. Keep buying the ground up shit you get at the Co-op. Para la gente mi amigo!!

Man, where's my head. Damn straight for the people. Hey, Petra is coming over in a bit. I have to change the sheets. I'll talk to you later.

Are we good? You know —about what happened in the 60's. I didn't mean to get you killed.

It's aigghht. Things could have been worse. Listen—you're a macho man like that G.

Com'on Che. I didn't have it like that. I'm not tryin' ta be a macho man. Whatever B. I thought you worked through that shit with your psycho-analyst?

Don't you dare bring up my psychoanalysis. I've worked too hard and long for you to unravel the work I've done with Shirley. Stick to video games, asshole.

Che! Com' on man. I didn't mean that. I don't want to fight. I can't deal with not talkin' for another five years. I just need to know that we're okay. Peace Che?

DAMN FIDEL! You do this all the time. I can't make a decision without seeing my psychoanalyst and she's out for a week. We'll talk then. Later.

TWO HOURS LATER

Petra? Hi, can I talk to Che? Thanks. Che—listen I know I'm not supposed to call till next week, but I'm stuck on level 9. Can't get past the Spectral Realm. Do I use the mist form?

You're a dumb mutha fucka. **OF COURSE YOU USE MIST FORM.** Damn! Talk in a week. Oh, make sure you pick up the extra health talisman behind the cross.

I knew I saw something behind the cross.

FIN

CRYING MACHO MAN
BY JOSÉ CABRERA

PEPY'S TAQUERIA

NOT ENOUGH CREAM CHEESE

TOASTED BAGEL

FIN

PEE SITTING DOWN

Che! I gotta question for you. Do you pee sittin' down or standin' up?

Amigo, you surprise me. What kind of man pees sitting down? I stand up—erect—like a macho.

Me too, like a **MACHO** man. I was just asking 'cause I got a cousin who pees sitting down. Can you believe that!?

Fidel, don't bullshit a bullshitter! Is Maria tellin' you to sit down? Damn Fidel, have some cojones!

Na-na. It's not like that! I-uh-well if you gotta know, my pee hole is mad big. Pee be splashing all over the place.

Har-ha I knew it! I still say a man should pee standin' up.

Whatever! At least I don't have to clean the bathroom every friggin' week.

...really?

Fidel might be on to something.

Pssssssssss

FIN

CRYING MACHO MAN
BY JOSÉ CABRERA

JUNGLE JUSTICE

FIN

SLICE OF PIZZA

FIN

THE JESUS BULLET

INFINITE SPACE

95

FIN

MADONNA AND CHILD

FIN

DRACULA WALKS INTO A LESBIAN BAR

Awww. Isn't he cute in his cape. He must be lost. **HEY CUTEY.** It's ladies night. How did you get in? Bruno is real strict on fag hags crashing the party.

Oh. Did I **OFFEND** you **COUNT**? Come on. You can hang out with me and my girlfriend.

Oh. Don't look at me like that. I don't dig guys. Haven't in 10 years. Never had an orgasm with a man.

CONT.

FIN